WHAT SHOULD I DO? WHAT SHOULD I DO?

COMMUNITY · CONNECTIONS
?

WHAT SHOULD I DO?
AT THE POOL

BY WIL MARA

3 1571 00299 4658

CHERRY LAKE
Publishing

Published in the United States of America by Cherry Lake Publishing
Ann Arbor, Michigan
www.cherrylakepublishing.com

Content Adviser: Karen Sheehan, MD, MPH, Children's Memorial Hospital, Chicago, Illinois

Photo Credits: Cover and page 5, ©Denise Mondloch; page 7,
©Susan Leggett/Dreamstime.com; page 9, ©Byron W. Moore/Shutterstock, Inc.;
page 11, ©Vahe Katrjyan/Shutterstock, Inc.; page 13, ©Helen & Vlad Filatov/Shutterstock, Inc.;
page 15, ©Poznyakov/Shutterstock, Inc.; page 17, ©Michael Walz/Dreamstime.com;
page 19, ©Starletdarlene/Dreamstime.com; page 21, ©Jane September/Shutterstock, Inc.

LIBRARY OF CONGRESS CATALOGING-IN-PUBLICATION DATA
Mara, Wil.
  What should I do? at the pool/by Wil Mara.
     p. cm.—(Community connections)
  Includes bibliographical references and index.
  ISBN-13: 978-1-61080-056-3 (lib. bdg.)
  ISBN-10: 1-61080-056-7 (lib. bdg.)
  1. Swimming for children—Safety measures—Juvenile literature.
  2. Swimming pools—Safety measures—Juvenile literature. I. Title.
  GV838.53.S24M37 2011
  797.2'1083—dc22   2011000131

Cherry Lake Publishing would like to acknowledge the
work of The Partnership for 21st Century Skills. Please
visit *www.21stcenturyskills.org* for more information.

Printed in the United States of America
Corporate Graphics Inc.
July 2011
CLFA09

AT THE POOL

CONTENTS

WHAT SHOULD I DO?

SWIMMING SHOULD BE FUN

It is fun to swim in a pool. You can play with your family and friends. Swimming is also very good for your body. But be careful! Pools can be dangerous. You should always follow the rules of pool safety.

Swimming pools are a great place to have fun and get some exercise.

Do you know how to swim? If not, ask your parents to sign you up for lessons. Knowing how to swim will be useful for your whole life.

5

MANY THINGS CAN HAPPEN

There are many ways to get hurt at a pool if you aren't careful. It is slippery on hard walkways and around the sides of the pool. It would be easy to fall if you ran.

Also remember that you cannot breathe underwater. You could **drown** if you stay under too long.

Being underwater is fun, but don't stay under too long!

How long do you think it takes to drown in a swimming pool? Ten minutes? Twenty? The answer is *less than five*. Your body needs air all the time. People cannot stay underwater for very long.

7

POOL RULES

Only go in a pool when an adult is nearby. This adult should be someone you know and trust. Make sure the adult is watching you. Say something to that adult if he or she is not watching. **Public pools** should always have **lifeguards** to watch you, too.

Lifeguards are good swimmers who know how to keep people safe at pools.

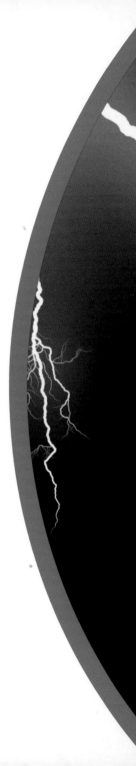

You wouldn't want to swim in a pool filled with dirty water. Don't go into pools that have just been cleaned with **chemicals**, either.

Do not swim in bad weather. Swimming during a thunderstorm can be dangerous.

If you see lightning or hear thunder, get out of the pool right away!

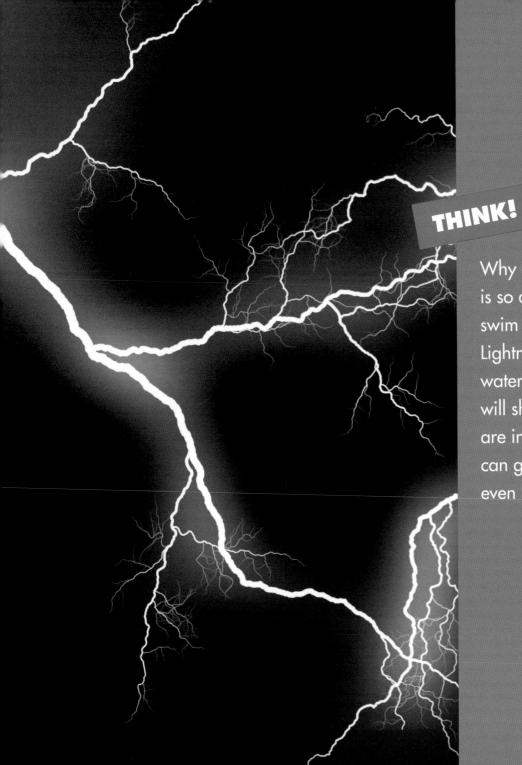

Why do you think it is so dangerous to swim during a storm? Lightning often hits water. The electricity will shock you if you are in a pool. You can get hurt or even killed.

11

RULES FOR SMART SWIMMERS

It is always a good idea to wear a **life vest** if you are not a strong swimmer yet. It will keep you from sinking. Life vests have kept many people safe in the water.

Life vests can help you stay safe in the water.

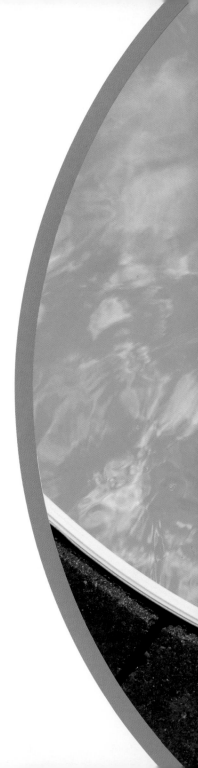

You should not fool around while you are at the pool. Do not push people. Don't throw things at friends who are in the water. Don't play on the ladders or the diving board.

Regular toys aren't made to be used in a pool. Only use floating pool toys. Remember not to ride your bicycle near a pool!

Be careful when using pool ladders. They can be slippery.

Look out for other children who are fooling around at a pool. Make sure you keep away from them. Ask an adult to stop them. These children can hurt you as easily as they can hurt themselves.

Only dive from a diving board. Always make sure an adult is watching when you dive.

Do not dive onto the pool toys or onto another person. Do not dive into the **shallow** end of the pool.

Never dive into shallow water. You could hit the bottom of the pool and hurt yourself.

Stay away from the pool's **filter** system. Do not put your hands near the filter **screens** that are underwater.

Do not go near the drains, either. You can get your hands or feet caught.

Only adults who are trained to take care of pools should ever go near filters and drains.

You probably don't feel like swimming when you are sick. Staying out of the pool is a good idea. That way you won't make anyone else sick.

Never go to the bathroom in the pool. Would you want to dive into a pool after someone did this? Of course not! It's a pool, not a bathroom!

You'll have fun at the pool and stay safe if you follow the rules.

GLOSSARY

chemicals (KEM-i-kuhlz) substances used to keep pool water clean

drown (DROUN) to die from breathing in water

filter (FIL-tur) a device that cleans liquids as they pass through it

lifeguards (LIFE-gahrdz) people who watch swimmers and help them if they are in danger

life vest (LIFE VEST) a soft piece of gear that fits onto your body to keep you floating in water

public pools (PUHB-lik POOLZ) pools that are open to anyone

screens (SKREENZ) sheets with very tiny holes that let water pass through but stop things such as leaves or pebbles

shallow (SHAL-oh) not deep

22

FIND OUT MORE

BOOKS

Knowlton, Marylee. *Safety Around Water*. New York: Crabtree Publishing, 2008.

Pancella, Peggy. *Water Safety*. Chicago: Heinemann, 2005.

Rau, Dana Meachen. *Water Safety*. New York: Marshall Cavendish Benchmark, 2010.

WEB SITES

KidsHealth—Swimming
kidshealth.org/kid/watch/out/swim.html
Read some safety tips for pools, lakes, and other places where you might swim.

PBS Kids GO!—Solo Sports: Swimming
pbskids.org/itsmylife/body/solosports/article4.html
Read about the ways swimming can make you stronger and healthier.

INDEX

ABOUT THE AUTHOR

Wil Mara is the award-winning author of more than 120 books, many of which are educational titles for children. More information about his work can be found at *www.wilmara.com.*

24

J
797.2108   Mara, Wil.
M   At the pool.

DATE			

BAKER & TAYLOR